THE GRAFFITI OF POMPEII

The Graffiti of Pompeii

Poems
by
LAURA SOBBOTT ROSS

Adelaide Books
New York/Lisbon
2018

THE GRAFFITI OF POMPEII
Poems
By Laura Sobbott Ross

Copyright © by Laura Sobbott Ross
Cover design © 2018 Adelaide Books

Published by Adelaide Books, New York / Lisbon
adelaidebooks.org

Editor-in-Chief
Stevan V. Nikolic

All rights reserved. No part of this book may be reproduced in any manner whatsoever without written permission from the author except in the case of brief quotations embodied in critical articles and reviews.

For any information, please address Adelaide Books
at info@adelaidebooks.org

or write to:

Adelaide Books
244 Fifth Ave. Suite D27
New York, NY, 10001

ISBN-13: 978-1-949180-62-6
ISBN-10: 1-949180-62-X

Printed in the United States of America

...from Puddle to her fishlet

Contents

I

    i.   (House of the Chaste Lovers)—*11*

II

    ii.   (exterior of the House of Menander)—*15*

    iii.   (in the basilica)—*17*

    iv.   (on the entrance to a private dwelling)—*19*

    v.   (above a bench outside the Marine Gate)—*22*

    vi.   (in the gladiator barracks)—*25*

    vii.   (on the House of the Moralist)—*27*

    viii.   (bar/inn joined to the Maritime Baths)—*29*

    ix.   (in the basilica)—*32*

    x.   (in the basilica)—*34*

xi. (Vicolo del Panattiere,
House of the Vibii, Merchants)—*36*

xii. (Street of the Theaters)—*38*

xiii. (Vico d' Eumachia,
small room of a possible brothel)—*40*

xiv. (Bar of Salvius; over a picture of
a woman carrying a pitcher of wine
and a drinking goblet)—*42*

xv. (stamp on a jar of garum)—*44*

xvi. (Bar of Athictus, to the right of the door)—*45*

xvii. (atrium of a House of the Large Brothel)—*46*

xviii. (Bar of Astylus and Pardalus)—*48*

xix. (Bar of Prima) [Written by Severus]—*50*

xx. (near the rear entrance vestibule of
the House of Menander)—*52*

xxi. (Samnite House)—*54*

xxii. (Inn of the Mule Drivers, left of the door)—*56*

xxiii. (in the gladiator barracks)—*58*

xxiv. (on the Salvius Inn)—*59*

xxv. (in the basilica)—*62*

xxvi. (House of Caecilius Iucundus)—*65*

xxvii.   (on a wall in the city)—**67**

xxviii. (House of the Calpurnii)—**68**

xxix.   (House of Caesius Blandus;
           in the peristyle of the House of Mars and
           Venus on the street of the Augustales)—**69**

xxx.   (in the basilica)—**70**

xxxi.   (written on a wall near the amphitheater)—**72**

xxxii.   (House of Hercules and Nessuss;
           beside the door of the house)—**74**

xxxiii. (on a wall in the city)—**76**

xxxiv.   (in the basilica)—**78**

xxxv.   (Nuceria Necropolis on a tomb)—**80**

xxxvi.   (next to an inscription of a phallus)—**82**

xxxvii. (on the street of Mercury)—**84**

xxxviii. (in the basilica)—**86**

xxxix.   (House of Poppaeus Sabinus; peristyle)—**88**

Acknowledgements   **91**

References   **93**

About the Author   **95**

I.

August 24, 79 A.D.

i. (*House of the Chaste Lovers*)

Remember the dances we shared together

A cold bath, a good book in the atrium,
the diarist noted of the August morning—
nothing uncivilized but the Roman sun
on the harbor town, and a curious cloud—
a gray-white bloom at the tip of the mountain.

The olive trees and the umbrella pines
shook with the rumblings of birds taking flight.
Ash began to drift— cloud-fray hissing
on clay tile roofs, the rope-led braying goats,
the vineyards, and the mouths of urns

shimmied from their footholds by a visceral
thunder, or hunger, to which the townspeople
showed indifference. After all, they'd chosen
to live exposed and on the edge. Sex and mountains—

Laura Sobbott Ross

ancient, feral landscapes.
    Both humanity and mythology
    frescoed in bawdy affirmations
across plaster walls. A naked contempt and nothing on

the altar of repentance but wine and fermented fish.
The sudden lambast of pumice, pockets of noxious wind,
        and everything else still
a mosaic, fragmented colors
postured into another climactic monument
to be admired from any stone couch in the domus.

Spare us your phallus, Artimus.
This sunrise has gone pitch.

Coitus and colonnades unmortised
from an exacted geometry—
the repertoire of: repeat, repeat, repeat,

even as the blue algorithms of the sea
recalibrated so precisely
that skates and eels were left writhing

on the sand, where schools of gasping mullet
were a silver fray on the hemline
of a blanket of roiling stone.

II.

No day shall erase you from the memory of time

—Vergil

ii. *(exterior of the House of Menander)*

Satura was here on September 3rd

Pompeii lies dying but doesn't know it.
The first blush of death,
an aching, exquisite sensitivity.
Its epicenter stirs open. In fields,
the wheat chafes and winces golden.
The mountain breathes and sweats in pearls
that bud. A fever has been born.
The animals nosing its warm bloom

at the edge of everything. The basalt soil,
black as tea grains, infuses the grass
with the ancient essence of smoke,
but green has never tasted so feral.
Soon, soon, call the mourning doves;

harvests of olives and grapes
will fill the presses, and dormice,

Laura Sobbott Ross

farmed and fattened for their winter sleep,
will be ready for roasting,
to be dipped and rolled
in more than just this honeyed light.

Don't try to catch them by the tails.
They're meant to be expendable—
a bit of furred flesh left twitching in your fist.

Where are you going, Satura?
I hope for your sake, the sea
is a headier calling than this city-bellus,
its coffers of lily and sex and wine.

Let it let go
of your wrists; its whispers
holy and hot in your hair. Unlock
its shiny gaze. Then, listen, Satura.
Can't you hear an ocean un-damning?

Soon, soon, call the voices from the ash
trees and the acacias. It's time to go.
Take your satchel of spells and pomegranates,
your good winter horse, and ride home.

iii. *(in the basilica)*

**Love dictates to me as I write and Cupid
shows me the way, but may I die if god
should wish me to go on without you.**

There were plenty of deities to choose from.
    The gods and goddesses of
war and love and death. And thunder,
and wine, keys, horses, and apricots.

Not to mention the one who first opens
the mouths of the newborns to cry.

And the punisher of broken promises.
    Some were lesser:
terrestrial and *indigitamenta:*
        divined, demi, and divi.
There was hardly a temple to spare
or a flame not already lit
with someone else's invocation:

a rib of linden, a small clay bell, a song thrush
with its throat slit. *Love lies bleeding* on the altar—

Laura Sobbott Ross

the name of a flower (Amaranthus caudatus).
A favorite of Venus? Or Clementia,
goddess of forgiveness and mercy?

Touch the shrine when you pray.
Listen for answers— auspices and omens.
The patterns of the pigeons. Your lover's small lies.

Seek favor first from the gods and the goddesses,
but wear your amulet just in case.
Avoid owls. Never host an even number of diners.
Always cross a threshold with your left foot first,

and pay attention to your dreams. Remember,
> even one of the Vestal Virgins of Rome
> was struck by lightning on her way home.

iv. (on the entrance to a private dwelling)

Oh, would that it were permitted to grasp with my neck your little arms as they entwine [it] and to give kisses to your delicate little lips. Come now, my little darling, entrust your pleasures to the winds. (En)trust me, the nature of men is insubstantial. Often as I have been awake, lovesick, at midnight, you think on these things with me: many are they whom Fortune lifted high; these, suddenly thrown down headlong, she now oppresses. Thus, just as Venus suddenly joined the bodies of lovers, daylight divides them and if...

Vesuvius embodied desire,
the townspeople knew it.
Like any other absolute:
Sun. Moon. Mountain. Death.

It loomed above the forum
and the amphitheater,
the peddled cabbages,
gold and leather at the marketplace,
the round portals of the thermal bath,
the Egyptian chain-gangs in the fields
of flax outside the city walls.

Laura Sobbott Ross

Dawn was an illumination.
Dusk, a silhouette.
Look at me, darling,

the onerous blue canvas crooned,
as if sketching the eyes that lifted
to swallow it daily in increments
of vineyard, basalt, & snow cap.
Vesuvius. The name,
a praise song. A curse.

Its inclines slick with shadow and cloud—
wandering currents rendered in
ghosted, trembling light. Oh heartbeat,
would it have made a difference
if the people of Pompeii had sacrificed
a virgin every year during the fire
festival of Vulcanalia? Someone's daughter
tipped into its wide mouth; a terrible
freefall in garlands and streaming girlish ribbons.

Lean in, mountain.
We want to know:
why do you need us?

You, with your own weather,
your tall shadow cast about us like a net.
Your god-perch so high we are nothing
but a small labyrinth of smoke and stone.
We, who are distracted and enviably alive.

v. (above a bench outside the Marine Gate)

**If anyone sits here, let him read this first of all:
if anyone wants a screw, he should look
for Attice; she costs 4 sestertii**

Was it enough to be willing
    to maintain the allure? Her face readied. The ninth hour
after sunrise, a palette of white marl, swan fat, rust, and soot—
a rim of stain around her eyes she mapped with a charred bit
of cork.

No lullaby on this bed of stone where she splayed—
a fillet of fine aching
bones, hennaed hair fanned across a pillow of straw,
her lips sliding

    into a simper. Sometimes the stars
    brought anguish, a mirror
of this city's small burnings. She wished for wine uncut by water,
for rosehips and olives and pomegranate,
       for sea urchin spooned from a pebbled shell.

Wasn't she famished?
After all, she was called *she-wolf* by the
men of Pompeii, those lesser gods
who drunkenly swore allegiance to Rome
before crossing the threshold of her
chamber, their swords already drawn
from a sheathe of foreskin.
> Her oiled curls unfollying. Her tunic,
> a current of grope and throttle.

The men were cruel or wildly grateful, bawdy or beguiled.
> Some chided their comrades in nearby
> chambers while otherwise
> > *occupatus* themselves. Her skin leaching the lead essence

of their crude tavern wines, a night's worth of dregs and resin.

> Still, she'd held the first fruits of the
> sons of Rome in her teeth
> more than once. See those patchwork
> curtains in her doorway?

They were sewn from the backs of their mothers' eyelids.
The flame in her

Laura Sobbott Ross

        oil lamp, a silent chant to Venus, a goddess so powerful
a whole man could slide, howling and repentant,
        into the corners of her eyes. On the other side of her

curtains, quiet slave boys, the *aquarioli*,
        who waited with cleansing water bowls in a
        Tyrrhenian wind
            that never trifled or hissed of recompense.
The moon, silver
and stamped with a man's laureled head.

vi. *(in the gladiator barracks)*

Antiochus hung out here with his girlfriend Cythera

Plunder sounds trunk-heavy, a spine of hinges that bite shut,
    soft bodies oathed into foreign armor.
    Look what the infantry dragged in:
        a spinner's slave and a warrior-in-training—
lovers combing ashes from their shiny hair. Grab your dagger

and your shield, Antiochus,
and that charging leopard by the throat.
    Today, the crowd adores you.
At this arena, they'll sell your sweat as an aphrodisiac
    and that beast's fat in smudge pots
    will carry the fingerprints of slave girls
earnest at the creases of their mistress's skin. Take up your

spindle, Cithera, your snags of linen and wool,
your longitudes & latitudes of warp and weft. What language

do you share? What blood? Iron and flax,
you can't mend the other. *Infamia,* remember everything

belongs to Rome. Like that basalt mountain
    Like that blue sea. *Your molars. Your tendons.*
    Like those bastions of olive & fig.
Your breath at the altar's flame. Like this reeking
sprawl of humanity poised on the hillside. *Every blistered seed
spring-loaded inside of you.* Like those small, bleating animals
ferried up the incline for the slaughter.

vii. *(on the House of the Moralist)*

Let water wash your feet clean and a slave wipe them dry; let a cloth cover the couch; take care of our linens

Our linens are everything. Decorum
laundered in sulfur and urine— urns of it,
tipped and stomped beneath the feet of slaves.
Splattered hemlines drying into a horizon

of sepia clouds. Stola, palla, tunic, toga—
we all need a soft place to fall.
Indian silk and linen. A nuzzle
against naked skin, folds to swallow
us in like dizzied bees in the atrium garden:
narcissus cupping April in yellows,
Tyrian purple, meant for dignitaries,
a status too upright for crocus—

the fragile tonguing at a sheen of new frost.
Pull on your wools and your sandals, Lucius.
Gather my crimson at the shoulder

Laura Sobbott Ross

with that pearl clasp, Cornelia. Mulsum,
a honeyed wine taken at the baths
not to be confused with muslin, an issue
dulled into the slaves' mustards and browns.

Throw wide the sun-dried bedsheets,
Faustina, and let them flutter and pool
at the edge of our dreaming.
Our cypress trees and poppy fields.
Our wrinkled blue lagoon. Our linens,
the voluminous map of this household's
slips & spoonings. Slave girls
with their spinnerets, mending, mending.

viii. (bar/inn joined to the Maritime Baths)

**Two friends were here. While they were, they
had bad service in every way from a guy named
Epaphroditus. They threw him out and spent 105
and half sestertii most agreeably on whores.**

—— Oil us up, Epaphroditus.
Is that what you said your name was?
These sausages are stale.
This wine tastes like vinegar.
Pour it out. But first, a toast:
to the dizzying mosaics, the floor tiles—
a tessellation ad nauseam. I'm bored

with colonnades and porticos.
Keep an eye on my clothes.
I need another towel. Why the scowl?
The mournful arches of your brows?
You're from Gaul? It sounds like bile—
the brown sedations steeped in my liver.

Ouch. Your fingers are biting
the sinews of my neck and shoulders.

Laura Sobbott Ross

They smell foul. Shield me from that
fat man's gluteus maximus.
See the shadow on the sundial?
More wine, did you hear us?

I've been iced.
I've been tepid.
I've been boiled.

Now, scrape me clean of this oil.
Clear my pores for the whores.
Raze my whiskers. Pluck my nose hairs.
Anything errant is yours. Consider it a tip.
My testicles itch. Is that clear?

No, not the wine, you fool!
Pick up the pieces of that platter.
What's the matter?
Epaphroditus, lean close. Closer still.
Your throat fits nicely in my fist.

When you sleep tonight
on your mattress of cobblestone,

——— remember this:
that hot howling and panting
you hear will not be the wind.

ix. *(in the basilica)*

Phileros is a eunuch!

He was too well versed in mythology and languages to pretend he believed his mother when she told him the word meant *unique*. So what if he spent his time in the atrium sketching parakeets at the fountain or the hoopoes among the scattered grains of emmer. Across the strings of his cithara, notes were pulled into the air in flourishes as fine as brushstrokes. He could sing an octave in alto. That small hand-knotted net on the bench beneath the myrtle tree was meant not for fish, but butterflies. *Both an iridescence*, he'd shrugged and noted to no one in particular. And when lunch was served at the sixth hour after sunrise, he preferred that his truffles and sardines didn't touch on the plate and insisted that a smear of cedar resin be kept in a small crock nearby to discourage insects. His mother fussed and pandered, invited daughters of high society friends to share a meal with them in the garden. *Teach me how to braid,* he whispered to Aquilina, the red-haired slave girl, her industrious fingers wrested from the peonies. Pulchritude and palindromes were his amusements:

```
M  A  S  K  S
A  P  E  E  K
S  E  X  E  S
K  E  E  P  A
S  K  S  A  M
```

Well, he hadn't quite figured that one out yet. There was nothing vulgar in patterns or archetypes. Science and classical geometry soothed him: the ordering of columns, spaces, and species. He kept a pair of greyhounds, dogs that looked like they were fighting a stiff wind. From his preened patch of hyssop and thyme, crushed fragrances in a silk pouch were pinned beneath his tunic. Even during the festival of Saturnalia every December, when the city unmasked into an incorrigible debauchery, he stayed home to offer prayers at the altar, not to Jupiter but to Cupid— that free flying boy-god with his quiver of unspoken intentions.

x. *(in the basilica)*

**Let everyone one in love come and see.
I want to break Venus's ribs with clubs
and cripple the goddess's loins. If she can
strike through my soft chest, then why
can't I smash her head with a club?**

I cannot defend myself, Venus.
    There is no armor for the heart.
    And if there was, it would be heavier than bronze,
and tooled with scenes of the victory processions
    of my former lovers. See their flaunted laurels?
    My histories portioned on their swords?
Everyone thinks you are a lady, Venus—
    incarnate of froth and abalone.
    But you are a savage
current tipped and conjuring a shore
    (meaning some dumb continent.)
    I know your ocean, Venus,
the shields of blue cabochon inside
    your wide, hopeful eyes, your perfumed undulations,
    your sheen on sheen of rollick and submerge.

Damn me for saying all this, Venus,
    or just send another pretty girl my way.
    What's the difference?

xi. *(Vicolo del Panattiere, House of the Vibii, Merchants)*

Figulus loves Idaia

On the altar of Venus, lay his offerings— cockles and sea star, dried tuberose, and a small bronze key that had emerged cleanly through a slit in the belly of a mackerel. The stars were a snarl of hooks and barbs through which his fingers patiently plodded until the shoals were visible at first light, drawn to the surface by the smell of cut bait. Fish traps rocked. A net was circumferenced in a rustic prayer circle of men. The sea still startling Figulus with its weathers and its alms: conger, lobster, sea urchin, octopus, cuttlefish, Idaia— the mermaid in his blood. Idaia attended a mistress who wore a wig of the finest blond of Germanian slave girls, and whose villa was as magnificent as a temple to the gods. How fitting for Idaia to be housed there! A flame point, the purest note of a siren song. Her braid, a thick black rope that swung from her shoulders as she knelt to shake out the folds of her mistress's silks and linens, and to fasten sandals over ankles oiled in cinnamon and myrrh. "Piscator!" That fine mistress spat the words at Figulus like a curse. Bangle bracelets on her wrists shuddering into her sleeves in a succession of O's. The pan-flute that enticed skates and crabs to the shore, paused at his thigh. Idaia's dark eyes, an ocean. At the threshold between them, he'd stood weeping fish scales and salt crystals from his skin like Icarus with his feathers and melted pitch—what a radiance he must have been, what an audacious spectacle of yearning.

xii. *(Street of the Theaters)*

A copper pot went missing from my shop. Anyone who returns it to me will be given 65 bronze coins (sestertii). 20 more will be given for information leading to the capture of the thief

Copper and fire are harmonious elements: metal and flame to which earthy rustics are added: olive oil, crushed mint leaves, honey, and the brine of fermented fish— garum, the essence of all things Roman. Just an ordinary, everyday pottage. Who knew that a simple medley could conjure a monkey? The wild, biting pet of Tuccius Antonius Augustinus, who'd stolen her from a street beggar in Rome. Chewing through a loosely braided basket of willow branches, the monkey washed and drank of the rainwater in the impluvium, then shimmied up a column of the peristyle. From there, she took to the interlocking roofs, where she hurled loose clay tiles onto the heads of pedestrians, who, not being able to see the source of the bombardment, hurried home to offer repentance at the altar of Mars. After dark, the monkey swung through the shop-keeper's window, and being hungry, licked at the pungent essences on the wall of the copper pot before taking a shit beneath a mosaic of cranes. She chewed down a clump of red grapes and a small bouquet of violets before easing the copper pot back out of the window to the roof where it fell onto the cambered stone below— a metallic note reverberating so distinctly against the dull grain of cicada, the shopkeeper stirred in his sleep. He would have found it there on the street next to his shop in the morning had the outflow from a strong spring rain not carried it into the storm drain and sent the monkey scrambling over the city wall into the shelter of an orchard of almond trees.

xiii. *(Vico d' Eumachia, small room of a possible brothel)*

Gaius Valerius Venustus, soldier of the 1st praetorian cohort, in the century of Rufus, screwer of women

I flaunt myself in three given names,
the earmark of Roman citizenship
— a fist of iron syllables drummed
against my armored breastplate.
See my swagger and know that I am

a soldier of the emperor's elite,
brawn and a royal kinship I can wield
more precisely than this diamond point,
double-edged gladius. Rufus?
A misplaced modifier. Don't you see it?

After all, it is I, Gaius Valerius Venustus
who is the screwer of woman, and he,
a philosopher in pursuit of virtue,
the keeper of a governance of restraint
I can only adhere to on my harbor city beat:

police, fire, crowd control at the stadium.
Make me an offer, shopkeeper.
Don't cut my wine with honey, barmaid.
I will surrender to nothing
but sexual pleasure. *Acquiesce*,

would make a good name for a whore.
Those pliable girls with their veins
of stinking foreign blood.
I can make their legs lock
around the flint contours of my torso,

the rollicking horizon of my back.
Beyond their cold, seductive smiles,
I could not tell you that their eyes
are an ache so bright
they could conjure fire.

xiv. *(Bar of Salvius; over a picture of a woman carrying a pitcher of wine and a drinking goblet)*

**Whoever wants to serve themselves can
go on and drink from the sea**

This wine's cut with water. In Pythagorean proportions.
Let all the Greeks raise their goblets.
Hail to mathematical scholars.
To the greatest philosophers. To architectural splendors.
Only barbarians drink undiluted wine.
Let all the Thracians raise their goblets.
Hail to everything beautifully uncivilized.
To the gods who likewise need no dilutions.
Romans have the most enchanting whores.
Let the Gauls raise their goblets.
And the Scythians. And the Thracians.
And the Germanians. And the Celts. Hail
to dice rolls and scattered knucklebones. Cast my lots.
Bring me olives and bread. No tantrum
or bloodied fist will land you
double sixes, Inebrius— only Venus herself,

but not in this reeking Hades.
Leave your empty amphoras on Neptune's
altar, your crockery and bronze.
This barmaid's sending us down to the sea.
Maybe the mermaids will satisfy your fetish
for fish, Tyberius. But, be wary:
that fermented mullet sauce in your beard will draw sharks.
Those floating lanterns of jellyfish
are Medusas with electric hair.
You can paw the sand over your
defecations like a cat, Marcellus.
Your gonads will float like an avocet.
The sea is a great equalizer,
Quintus, no, not a great elixir.
Leave some coins by these drained goblets,
lest we wake tomorrow on the rasping beach pebbles,
with seawater, sharp and scolding, on our shriveled tongues.

xv. *(stamp on a jar of garum)*

Kosher garum

Ingredients: nothing tentacled; or tongue-footed, no limpets un-nippled from hulls or moorings; no carapaces, no claws or otherwise expendable appendages; nothing viscous or mucous or prone to nacreous extrusions of pearl; no siren or fossil; nothing segmented or arrayed, ciliated or ink-glanded, egg cased or undulating; nothing floating, nothing pinioned; nothing larvaed in stages like insects— thoraxed and parasitic; nothing electric or wing-spanned or fanged; dorsal: yes, but finned only; eyes upon death that were clear and bright; scales, once removed that didn't tear the skin. Herein putrefies only that which died forthwith un-netted and flapping; the galled gizzard gut rot of mackerel, mullet, anchovy (or approved equivalent), brined and festering beneath a potent Roman sun.

xvi. *(Bar of Athictus, to the right of the door)*

I screwed the barmaid

The barmaid responds:
As if your conquests were worth the wall space, patron.
However small. Your tally, I mean. Wink, wink. If you
feel the need to boast— bravo for your bravado. Take that
fig-sized bit of plaster between the vining clematis and
the endorsement for Aedile and scratch your braggadocio
right where it itches. Can you find it? Do you feel
better now? Yawn. Well, there's my footnote, patron. To
be honest, I really don't remember you. You and your
drunken brethren are one in the same to me— a cavern
of grunt and prod and fish sweat and oily wicks where
you squabble over knucklebones and bloodied dice as
if they were bread and air. But I would wager that what
you meant by screwed, was screwed over. As in coins
that were never procured for your watered-down wine.
Patron, what do you think it was watered down with?

xvii. *(atrium of a House of the Large Brothel)*

Blondie has taught me to hate dark haired girls. I shall hate them if I can, but I wouldn't mind loving them. Pompeiian Venus Fisica wrote this.

The Pompeiian dreams of his goddess— Venus Fisica. Funny how she thinks like him. She's whimsical and loves bells, he's decided and tells everyone he knows. The prostitutes at the Lupinar laugh at this, especially the dark-haired ones who shim their loose curls inside muslin ribbons and stroke their throats in lily root and lead. Every Pompeiian knows that Venus loves swans and doves and pretty white things like lambs. And she loves love. Even procured love. Certainly, the goddess is blonde, he's decided. With hair like the downy hollow of a bird nest. And eyes that are eggshell blue. He tells them that she's very gay in the old-fashioned sense of being heedlessly blissful. That she wears a charm that is a phallus. Because she favors men, of course. And brothels and fertility and babies, but not necessarily in that order. *She was born on the sea, you know,* he says. *We know,* they say, fidgeting with their toes, adjusting their tunics, or lolling around with their chins resting in their girlish hands. Musettes, all. Roses, who bind his cuts and scrapes with tensile spider webs, and who think sneezing after sex will keep them from getting pregnant; the air, thick with pollen. Oh, how Venus loves a garden. After all, he reminds them, she's the only immortal to be rendered of simple earth, fevered from a gravity that swelled into a current that blissed into a woman. The girls watch the horizon. The clouds are a froth. *Does she have wings*, one of them asks.

xviii. *(Bar of Astylus and Pardalus)*

**Lovers are like bees in that they
live a honeyed life**

The hexagon in a honeycomb
    is a geometric perfection.
    Nature's golden ratio.
A waxy tessellation of industry & sex.
    Honey, come home.
    There's an audible buzz
in the hive. I've gone nectared.
    Honed to a node keening like a queen bee,
    you & I are a tightly threaded orbit
whose loose ends loll
    in the pollen of apricot, lily, and thyme.
    The butterflies are drunk on us.
Even the snails are gorged—
    plump and sugared.
    Honey, pour me some more.

I'm dizzled and dazzy.
    This instinct's sweet.
    An amber drizzle on our tongues.
If only we could bottle it.
    Keep it for our own. Hold its gold
    up to the light.

xix. *(Bar of Prima) [Written by Severus]*

Successus, a weaver, loves the innkeeper's slave girl named Iris. She however does not love him. Still, he begs her to have pity on him. His rival wrote this. Goodbye. [Response by Successus] Envious one, why do you get in the way. Submit to a handsomer man and one who is being treated very wrongly and good looking. [Response by Severus] I have spoken. I have written all there is to say. You love Iris, but she does not love you.

Don't look at your reflection, cautioned Attilia, the guardian of the boy. *Revere the nuances.* Oracle, sage, specularii— the boy at the black mirror was an orphan taken in by the widow, a mid-wife whose hands shook despite her youth. He'd arrived in the shadow of an owl at the Salt Gate of the city with an incantation in his baby teeth. Reading the patterns of birds, he could predict death and birth and betrayal as told to him in wing and song. An ache in his wrist bones meant a sky of horsetail clouds. Sometimes he'd pin moths open and channel the wide, soft eyes of their wing spots. He was too tenderhearted to read the entrails of sheep and goats like other mystics; he'd become seized with the sad disquietude

of their slaughter. Attilia believed he might be the collective soul of the babies she'd lost while helping the women of Pompeii give birth. An unburdening of grief she could nourish into a man. In the custom of the Etruscans, the boy as best at scrying mirrors. Set like a bowl of water on a table, the black mirror was a portal between two oceans: the living and the dead. At its glass skin, spirits surfaced and spoke in watery articulations, a ghostly undercurrent in their limbs. It was a warm night. *Cold air can lead to pondering,* Attilia had noted. Iris needed to choose between two men, the boy said finally, his head of curls curiously angled as he gleaned the obsidian glow: *The weaver and the barber. Both names hiss, a riotous competition. This triangle, to quote the Greeks, is an isosceles, in which only two of the sides match precisely. One of them is you, of course,* he nodded at Iris, *& the other…* Iris caught her breath, and leaning closer, glimpsed the image of a cloud and a cobalt mountain reflected in the mirror before them. The boy gasped and choked and recoiled:
Fire! Fire! Fire! Fire!

xx. *(near the rear entrance vestibule of the House of Menander)*

At Nuceria, look for Novellia Primigenia near the Roman gate in the prostitutes' district

Novellia Primigenia was past her prime.
Likely thirty, maybe more. She was garishly optimistic—
a canvas of coal, and white lead face paint
that made her teeth appear more yellow than they were.

The boys had learned not to kiss her skin
because its poisons
could accumulate in the marrow of their bones.

Novellia swaddled her heavy breasts to her ribs
as if there were nursing babies at her nipples.
After all, breasts were not for pleasure
but for the sustenance of children
(and these men weren't?)

She smelled humid, of fennel and seawater.
An oily ripened rose.

THE GRAFFITI OF POMPEII

She was well versed in Vergil: *instead of a long skirted gown,*
a tiger's spoils hang down her back.

Her hair was a dark mountain fashioned with a coronet
riveted in seed pearls that looked like baby teeth.
She could leer with her laugh
and thought herself to be an epic mime and muse,
and an even better lover. Beside a flame,
she kept a bowl of trinkets. Small offerings at her own altar—
jeweled bits of minutia traded for favors of a sensual nature

She-earth. Goddess of her body, it's generous, reckless yield.
Oh, the way these boys fell wincing
into her skin! Their praises
exhaled stale with wine and heat
in an all too brief moment of toe-curling exaltation.
It was what she lived for.

xxi. *(Samnite House)*

[Caricature of a woman with horns, claws, teeth, and wings, holding a scythe or staff]

As I pass through fields of wheat, insects shrivel and drop from the stalks, but only if my hair and bodice are wild and loose, and I am barefoot, but not at dawn. Because at dawn, everything in my wake could die. Or so the scholars say. You see, a menstruating woman is potent. Purple loses its luster in my presence, and mirrors go dull. Bees abandon their hives, and the tendrilled vinelings of grapes wither to dust, so don't ask me for honey or wine. And to the men: run. Especially if there is an eclipse, lest I seduce you into something that will release in you distillations of poison or insanity, for I am no doubt in a fatal state of grace. By that I mean, this period. In which I can stop hailstones, whirlwinds, lightning, birth. I've been told to carry a small, red fish to temper my powers. Still, dogs will go mad. The linens I boil turn black. Copper pots rot and verdigris. Even tar will dissolve at my bidding. But remember, I am medicinal, a nurturer by nature. So, mix the ash of my monthly courses with the oil of roses, soot, and wax, and apply me to boils, headaches, and fevers. Protect yourself from curses and magicians, phobias and seizures. But beware the essences of a woman of a questionable nature, and don't stand with us beneath a tree heavy with apples and thorns, or a sky of simple stars.

xxii. *(Inn of the Mule Drivers, left of the door)*

**We have wet the bed, host.
I confess we have done wrong.
If you want to know why,
there was no chamber pot**

There was no party like a party in Pompeii:
Lupercalia, Ludi Floridales, Saturnalia.
Sun city, sin city on the Mediterranean,

a festival every month. The Vestal Virgins
in Rome industrious at their ovens,
baking ceremonious breads and cakes.

The prostitutes, a bawdy gravity
next to sideshows of weary oddities.
Exotic animals hungry and waiting

to be uncaged before the crowds
at the amphitheater. Another theme,
another aficionado releasing

the chariot racers from their mark.
Morning, a sticky residue

of vomit and spilled wine. Wilted garlands

still festooning the necks of donkeys.
Bonfires pooled into silver ash.
Bloodied altars that smell like rust.

The ancestral spirits would be quelled
back into their graves for now.
Amphoras refilled with oil and honey and cream.

There were dusty peacock feathers to be gathered.
Poultices to be brewed for the evil eye.
The slaves sweeping up bones and shards,

and dragging fouled artifacts into the sun
while the drunks and the gods rose again,
thirsty, and blinking back the light.

xxiii. *(in the gladiator barracks)*

I made bread

No matter how you slice it, it's a metaphor
risen from stone once hot as an oven floor.
Wit or wheat? Bulgur or vulgar? *Excretus*—
roughhewn and dusted in a fine farina of ash.

xxiv. *(on the Salvius Inn)*

Come and drink with us, Oceanus

It doesn't matter that you are a Greek,
Oceanus, wine is a great equalizer.
So is being a gladiator.
Is it true that a violent earthquake
shook you from your mother's womb?
What's it like to be locked in the eyes of a lion?
Both are the same as living in Rome
as a Greek slave, you say.

Barmaid, more falernian for this champion.
Let us feed you, Oceanus.
Let us fatten you for the kill.
By that we mean your scorecard of beasts,
of course, the leopards and the bears,
the Thracians and the Samnites
wielding honed bronze. Drunk

Laura Sobbott Ross

under the cool awnings in the amphitheater,
we will swoon for you, Oceanus, your blood
on our tongues. If you win, we will lay our alms
at your feet, our laurels and silver. A ticket out?

Your eyes do cling to the horizon—
the quicksand sea, and that high wall
of mountains. Yes, yes, a toast before you go
back to your cell. *Ave imperator, morituri te salutant!*
(Hail emperor, we who are about to die, salute you!)

One last thing, Oceanus, tell us about the women.
The ones who sit so close you can feel them
keening through the blood in your eyes,
their vestments trimmed in royal purple,
those wives and daughters of noblemen.

It's like throttling Rome to the bone, you say.
Your teeth at its soft pampered throat,
its submissively splayed limbs,
and fatted underbelly. *To the victor,
go the spoils*, and you're right,

these are the words of one of our own.
Brothers, this Greek slave quotes
our great Caesar to his own benefit.
Yes, well, laughter is a great equalizer,
Oceanus, but so is death.

xxv. *(in the basilica)*

**Take hold of your servant girl whenever
you want to; it's your right**

Said a man with a servant girl.
        Maybe she was the one
buying leeks and apples for his wife
in the marketplace.
        Or maybe she was

the wet nurse, or the girl who gave lessons
      in Greek to his children,
braided their hair, and kept them
        rapt with mythology
whispered during thunderstorms.

Maybe she was the one
        whose long, pretty fingers
smelled like spices picked fresh
from the atrium garden:
        rue and sage and pennyroyal.

The one who held the mirror. The one
who oiled the sandals, and bled
the honeycombs. The one who dumped
his chamber pot daily into the street.
    The one who avoided his eyes

when he watched her hungrily
        while she swept the ashes
for the morning fire,
humming something softly foreign.

Maybe she was thinking of the last time
she saw her mother in Antioch,
        her eyes long-journeyed
and shot through with aquamarine light.
Or about her baby sisters,

        flushed and sweet.
Or about the Roman soldiers,
and how the medallions on the long leather fringe
of their belts had clacked in the cavalcade
like an iron chant.

Laura Sobbott Ross

Or about the first time she had seen snow.
        How it stunned her skin
and her vision. As if the dome of the sky itself
        had fractured and sifted

into fragile drifts. A strange numbness
erasing the landscape of her childhood
in clean, white stitches.

xxvi. *(House of Caecilius Iucundus)*

Whoever loves, let him flourish. Let him perish who knows not love. Let him perish twice over whoever forbids love.

There's always wind here,
        an audible current,
      a low rumbling at the monolith
    of these limestone footings.

Small offerings shimmy across altar floors.
      In the myrtle trees,
    pinfeathers stir on huddled songbirds.

Cascade:
    the dimpled wrists of cherubs
        tipping amphoras into trickles,
            pergola vines snaking lattice,

        ornamental trees gone vulgar
        with womb-heavy fruit.

Laura Sobbott Ross

Guard dogs are the guttural-speak of sensory intuition.
    Who else sits awake at the open window?

The night smells like smoke and pestilence.
Raised street stones are traced in shiny rivulets
of reeking waste.

That horizon of mountains is swallowing constellations whole.
    Tell me, who do you love?   What do you love?
        At wet frescos,
            squirrel hair brushes
      dandered in paint will repair nuances
        of weather and time.

Every stroke, an evolution.
    Candid murals cure in the teeth
        of mosaics—
matter fragmented, then rearranged again,
            one iota at a time.

xxvii. *(on a wall in the city)*

So may you forever flourish, Sabina; may you acquire beauty and stay a girl for a long time

When the baby was placed by the midwife next to a patch of narcissus and lilies in the grotto, moonlight made urgent by the shifting of clouds, left a thread of static that skimmed the hair and shoulders of a statue of Venus. Fish arced at once beyond the skin of the atrium pond as a current rippled through the baby's limbs. It was not unlike that of a sea urchin on the ocean floor, noted the patriarch of the household as he gathered the infant in his arms. It was a sign, he thought, picking wet petals from her skin. It meant they would keep her, even though she was a girl and the youngest of seven. The mother and her slaves, clasping and unsteadied, had wept with relief. Father and daughter, a culmination— skin on skin. She had studied his white hair, the whipping hemline of his cloak. Her own moonlit god. There was something worldly in her eyes, he'd decided as she sucked her fists, chilled and longing for her mother's breasts. The salt breeze, a lullaby that rocked the cypress and obelisks of ivy as her father held her up to the stars and named her for the ancients— his mother's own tribe of warriors.

xxviii. *(House of the Calpurnii)*

Crescens is sweet and charming

One was an architect & one, a gladiator. Both commissioned by Rome for the restoration of Pompeii in the big earthquake's wake. Each possessed a skilled trade that no one could dispute; there were peristyles to be aligned, & crowds to draw across the structural cracks in the ellipse of the amphitheater—*Sweet and charming?*—Crescens, with his proportional compass rendering geometric planes, and Crescens, armored with not much more than his trident and his net, taking down tigers. Women & columns swooning. The knots in a field of mesh no less ordered than the marble ribs of a colonnade. Each Crescens, the root and the rising wave in *crescendo*. Their charge— a spectacle, *spectacula*: the studious Greek delegating brawn into stone spandrels of arches, and the dark Hebrew with curls like onyx bells and a smile that could split flesh into a raucous chant and cloudbursts of laurel petals.

xxix. *(House of Caesius Blandus; in the peristyle of the House of Mars and Venus on the street of the Augustales)*

It took me 640 paces to walk back and forth between here and there ten times.

Here	4 + 4 + 4 + 4	4 + 4 + 4 + 4	4 + 4 + 4 + 4
	4 + 4 + 4 + 4	4 + 4 + 4 + 4	4 + 4 + 4 + 4
X	4 + 4 + 4 + 4	4 + 4 + 4 + 4	4 + 4 + 4 + 4
	4 + 4 + 4 + 4	4 + 4 + 4 + 4	4 + 4 + 4 + 4

4 + 4 + 4 + 4	4 + 4 + 4 + 4	4 + 4 + 4 + 4	4 + 4 + 4 + 4
4 + 4 + 4 + 4	4 + 4 + 4 + 4	4 + 4 + 4 + 4	4 + 4 + 4 + 4
4 + 4 + 4 + 4	4 + 4 + 4 + 4	4 + 4 + 4 + 4	4 + 4 + 4 + 4
4 + 4 + 4 + 4	4 + 4 + 4 + 4	4 + 4 + 4 + 4	4 + 4 + 4 + 4

4 + 4 + 4 + 4	4 + 4 + 4 + 4	4 + 4 + 4 + 4	
4 + 4 + 4 + 4	4 + 4 + 4 + 4	4 + 4 + 4 + 4	ψ
4 + 4 + 4 + 4	4 + 4 + 4 + 4	4 + 4 + 4 + 4	
4 + 4 + 4 + 4	4 + 4 + 4 + 4	4 + 4 + 4 + 4	There

xxx. *(in the basilica)*

**Sarra, you are not very nice,
leaving me all alone like this**

Everything has an epicenter,
a single point of origination
from which an impetus keens
open, chases itself in ripples that cease
to touch until they are dead as foam—
a tremble disassembling. See this town
square, these men and women navigating
in folds— tunic, and familia, both
a tight weaving of threads. Look
at the faces of the crowd. Can you see
the howl gone dormant in their molars?
The instinct for flesh. To lie down next to.
To penetrate. To be penetrated by.
These mountains are god-fisted, this sea
teems with a mercurial underpinning,
and at that shop I can buy seven

different kinds of olives, and at this one,
leather to lace my hobnailed soles.
No pole star necessary; I am oceaned
with humanity and imperatives.
If I let go of this stone door well,
I will swirl and eddy into the drift.
But loneliness, Sarra?
It is marrowed inside of us like air.

xxxi. *(written on a wall near the amphitheater)*

You have failed at times, but you could have failed sixteen times. You have drifted from job to job: innkeeper, baker, farmer, book binder, parts seller, junk dealer. You've done it all. Now, you're a pot maker's hand. Where are you headed?

Give them bread and circuses,
the politicians say.
One's taste for blood and grain
in this kingdom pacified
at no charge by Nero (all hail).
The crest of Rome inscripted
on every oven door and iron blade
thrust into the heart. Cattle, we the masses.
Left to wander, but not hungry, really.
The swivel of our once watchful eyes
locked in rust, our taste buds distilled
to a governmental issue— a fat wafer
void of anything honeyed or gamey.
Or of conquest. Or coveted. And savagery?
At a distance, it goes dull. Another processional
bleeding into a horizon of blue mountains

and sparkly seas where scattered bread crusts
are foraged by birds and foreigners.
Romans have the softest skin.
It's the public baths, the slaves readied
with the strigil at our shoulder blades
to scrape away our daily portion
of oil and dust before the plunge
into frigid water satisfies the longing
to be jolted awake. Call me home, master.
Where is the shepherd snapping at my heels?
Where is the bell and the mud braided path?
The smoke rising from the coals?
The bald prong of the moon?

xxxii. *(House of Hercules and Nessuss;
beside the door of the house)*

**Learn this: while I am alive, you,
hateful death, are coming.**

Once they were wild on the savanna, the wind carrying the scent of blue stem grass and wild melon. Always, there was the itch of hunger and thirst, but also the familiar earth of each other's skin. The darkness alert with mosquitos and stars. Every scant tree, a sculpture in thorn. Even the dusk was a blood orange latitude. Suddenly captured, they found themselves over water. Days at sea, a humid film of urine and salt. Zebras, lions, elephants, giraffes cowering in the corners of their crates, were too wild-eyed to notice their captors, or to dream or eat. Savage? That depends on your interpretation of the word. Weeks later, caged in Pompeii, they were kept ravenous, and prodded with spear points into a state of rage. *Come and see the kennel of exotics*: hyenas and tigers and bears. Ostriches. Crocodiles. Instincts heightened to a breaking point: the show before the show down. Almonds and gravel hurled sharply by taunting boys. Fanged scowls that were met with spit and jeers. At night, the pitiful wailing and pleading of the animals seeped into the dreams of the people of Pompeii. A mournful cacophony that stunted the moon and the mountain. Blood, a palpable essence, the iron taste of mo(u)rning. Everyone knew that at the next festival, all those gamey fillets would be divvied up among the bystanders after the choreographed kill. The sand floor swirled in blood and cheers, hoisted out again into the sea.

xxxiii. *(on a wall in the city)*

Nothing can last forever; once the sun has shown, it returns beneath the sea. The moon once full, eventually wanes, the violence of the winds often turns into a light breeze.

It's always a fine night for a funeral.
First, there is the music—
a cacophony of sorrow intuited.

Then, the professional mourners,
paid to lament loudly, to toss
their tears across the gathering crowds
on either side of the street.

A bit of salt and grief for your tunic, neighbor.

All hail, Hades, here come the death masks!
Face of the corpse interned in wax
and populating the city blocks,
as if the whole underworld were released
in a singular ghosting or that same damn moon.

Hide the eyes of your children, Mamma.

That portable platform shouldered by slaves
holds the body itself, biting down hard
on a coin that guarantees its passage
—— the metallic taste of a last request.

Remember, no bones
are allowed within these city walls.
Those old mountains are full
of funeral pyres

—— flames that rise high enough to lick the clouds,
and leave nothing
but charred bits of fossil for the urn—
voices of the dead that still speak in the ashes.

xxxiv. *(in the basilica)*

**Oh walls, you have held up so much tedious graffiti that
I am amazed you have not already collapsed in ruin.**

If only they'd known the centuries it would endure.
Self-preservation scratched into a canvas
of soft plaster with a bit of verve and moonlight.
Such a reckless entombment—riches like these:

Hectice, baby, Mercator says hello to you.

Random licks of more than simple Roman nomenclature,
or the platitudes and gratitudes of an era.

Aufidius was here.
Ash is a velvet curtain—
a magician's subtle wrists.
Snap the hemline, and let it float.
See how the antiquities gleam beneath it.

A kiosk of epitaphs:
whom to vote for,
whom to sleep with,

where to buy your bread
and fermented fish sauce.

Marcus loves Splendusa.

And he always will.
The naked affirmations of lovers,
a finer lilt than any brittle stylus.
Cruel Lalagus, why do you not love me?

These walls are still standing, after all,
beneath a confetti of etchings,
no translation necessary.
To whoever is defecating here,
someone writes, be forewarned
of a curse and the wrath of Jupiter.

There's a menacing hum in the air.
Lick your finger and touch
the space behind your ear.
Take the shortest route home.
A throng of voices is rising.

(Pyrrhus to his colleague Chius):
*I'm sorry to hear that you have died,
and, so, goodbye.*

xxxv. *(Nuceria Necropolis on a tomb)*

Greetings to Primigenia of Nuceria. I would wish to become a signet ring for no more than an hour, so that I might give you kisses dispatched with your signature

If love was a stylized motif,
it would be nothing
as simple as acanthus leaves—
fluted and fruited and voluted
in stone and blown sideways
at the tops of columns
by architectural winds; no,
it would be your name.
No chisel needed
beyond the heart-opus
of a blood ardor in simpatico—
the *ba-boom ba-boom ba-boom*
of a craftsmanship too vast
and ornate for any template of
wax or ivory or travertine or sky.

Heat holding its shape. To coalesce,
more or less. This tongue,
a rudimentary stylus on a
razed substrate of bread and horse
and tree and stars and oxygen,
your wrist, your throat, your thighs.
My signum to your sigillum.
Translated: signed & sealed here.
& here.   & here.   & here.   & here.
And   oh, yes, again,   here.

xxxvi. *(next to an inscription of a phallus)*

Handle with care

Mutunus Tutunus was a god in the form of a penis.
He was hung
sometimes with bells from a windchime
called a tintinnabula—
an onomatopoeia for the clapper in the bowl,
well, that's what you called the parts
when they swung in the wind—tin-tin,
slang for testicles. *Fascinum* or *fascinus*,
depending on your perspective.
Oh, those phallic charms (that's what she said)
were a remedy for invidia— just a simple case
of the evil eye. After all, in this Roman heat,
those words were a rudimentary reminder:
handle *with care*— *mansueta* (a lotta)
but not so mucha in the breezy

hemline of his toga. But, back to the god
who was his own throne of stone, his own
disclaimer, and potently spawning a multitude
of effigies cast in bronze and brawn.

xxxvii. *(on the street of Mercury)*

**Publius Comicius Restitutus stood
right here with his brother.**

On a street called mercury
              (or was it mercy)

in the quick silvered light,
two brothers watched the sea change.

A shifted weight, opalescent blue
to dark sapphire, while candle flames
thumbed up on wicks across the city.

It was a restive evening—
            a collective breath drawn and held.

The soles of the brothers' sandals
were wearing thin, but the coins
in their hands were an irresistible gravity.
They followed the stone medallions
of phalluses in the walkways.

Smoke lingered, residual of a celebration
or an attenuated hunger.

On the basalt hillside, succulents bloomed.
Horses tugged at their leads. Stray dogs
tunneled in the wild asparagus,
rolling themselves into heady scents.

Even the *lenos* and their charge—
the ladies of the night at the Lupinar,
were whimsical and distracted:
> *Warmest regards from Puddle to her fishlet.*
> Above the canted street,

Publius's brother pointed out the seabirds circling madly,
the whole lagoon thrashing and scaled in moonlight.

xxxviii. *(in the basilica)*

A small problem gets larger if you ignore it

*VE*STRA, VESTER, VESTRUM—	Yours—
VEGRANDRIS, VESTIGUM:	small relics, traces:
VENEA,	vineyard,
VOMER,	plowshare,
VENALICIUM, VIA,	market, road,
VICINUS,	neighbor,
VITA, VINUM VERIDIS.	wide, green life.
VALLUM.	Pompeii: palisade, earthen wall, entrenchment, rampart.
VESPER.	Evening star.
VIGILIO	And while you're looking up keep your eye out

VENTIO VIS.	for what might be coming next, especially regarding the forces of nature.
VAE. VADO.	Uh-oh. Hurry.
VOCO	Summon
VENIA,	grace, favor from the gods, a pardon,
VERTUS,	courage,
VEL	or
VERITAS:	the truth:
VESUVIO,	Mount Vesuvius
VESUVIO—	(remains) unextinguished—
VALDE, VEHEMENTER,	intensely, forcefully,
VORACIOUS	voraciously so.

xxxix. *(House of Poppaeus Sabinus; peristyle)*

If you felt the fires of love, mule-driver, you would make more haste to see Venus. I love a charming boy; I ask you, goad the mules, let's go. Take me to Pompeii where love is sweet.

The passenger
I am thinking of a crescent of light on the lower lid of his eye that's so fine I'd have to paint it with just a single whisker from a cat. Skin like milk. His tongue, a hook, and I am both ocean and a flitting iridescence, dull-eyed and ravenous. These clouds become a torso beneath this artist's hands, equal parts impetus and desire, hard as marble. Oh, I am blindsided tonight by more than just the sparks that float on wings across the vetch and briar. My secrets smolder deliciously. If it wasn't for the primitive weight in my loins, well, these old bones could fly.

The driver
I will get a fine wage tonight. In Pompeii, there will be bread and oil and fish. Perhaps a pottage or a whore. The sky silvers, and silhouettes of trees trudge by us on a landscape that is anything but linear. A tooth aches in my head like

a premonition. I touch the amulet of green jasper at my throat and think of werewolves. Funny how the melancholy smell of smoke is not a geography but a holy grain in everything. How old is the moon, I wonder. Does it burn?

The mules
A cadence, the cane. Impel, a good name for a mule. Or a driver. This mile carries the distant scent of cypress and fennel. The last one, the salt sea. I can lose myself in a rhythm. This small ache, that jag of hunger. My bones rattle and conspire. I taste iron but long for spring chaff and rivers. On a small sclera behind my retinas I sense flame. My ears swivel and hone to map its distant current. The green of leaf and blade already lick hotly at my limbs while smoke hisses from my pores. I will be tethered, hitched, whipped, and heavily burdened with your imperatives, caretaker, but I will not walk through fire. I won't burn for Pompeii.

Acknowledgements

For my students, all of whom teach me so much.

Many thanks to Lynne Davis Spies for her helpful edits on many of these poems. Brava!

I am grateful to the editors of the following publications in which these poems are forthcoming or herein first appeared, some in slightly different form:

Newfound: *i.* 2017

Mudlark: *ii., iii., ix., xiv., xviii., xx., xxi., xxx., xxxi., xxxix.,* 2018

References

Benefiel, Rebecca R. (2013-2018) "A Digital Resource for Studying the Graffiti of Herculaneum and Pompeii" The Ancient Graffiti Project; Retrieved in 2017 ancientgraffiti.org

Cartwright, Mark (November 18, 2012) "Pompeii Graffiti, Signs & Electoral Notices" Ancient History Encyclopedia; Retrieved in 2016 https://www.ancient.eu/article/467

Harvey, Brian "Graffiti from Pompeii" Pompeiana.org; Retrieved in 2016 www.pompeiana.org/Resources/AncientGraffitifromPompeii.htm

Heaphy, Linda (April 19, 2017) "The Bawdy Graffiti of Pompeii and Herculanium" Kashgar; Retrieved in 2017 https://kashgar.com.au/blogs/history/the-bawdy-graffiti-of-pompeii

Mommsen, Theodor (1861)
    Corpus Inscriptionum Latinarum, Volume 4; Berlin:
    Berlin-Brandenburgische Akademie der Wissenschaften.

Nadeau, Sophie (December 10, 2016)
    "Oh, Just Some 2000-Year-Old Graffiti from Pompeii"
    Solo Sophie Travel & Culture; Retrieved in 2017
    https://www.solosophie.com/graffiti-from-pompeii-italy

About the Author

Laura Sobbott Ross teaches English to ESOL students at Lake Technical College in central Florida, and has worked as a writing coach for Lake County Schools. Her writings appeared in Blackbird, Meridian, The Florida Review, Calyx, Natural Bridge, and many others. She was named as a finalist for the Art & Letters Poetry Prize 2016, and won the Southern Humanities Auburn Witness Poetry Prize 2017. Laura has been nominated four times for a Pushcart Prize. Her poetry chapbooks are A Tiny Hunger, and My Mississippi.